ICE
CREAM

Written and photographed
by William Jaspersohn

MACMILLAN PUBLISHING COMPANY
NEW YORK

The author wishes to thank Ben Cohen and Jerry Greenfield, and all the employees, past and present, at Ben & Jerry's, who helped make this book possible. Extra-special thanks to Diane Elliott, Dave Barrish, Chico Lager, Jim Miller, Scott Sandifer, Laurie Rowe, Alyssa Rowe, and Laurie Sicard at Ben & Jerry's; Dan Regan and Mike Fowler at the Amstar Sugar Refinery, Charlestown, Massachusetts; Bernard LaRose and his fellow workers at the St. Albans Cooperative Creamery, St. Albans, Vermont; George Pigeon and his family, and Michael Gaudette in St. Albans; Halsey Kendricks and Liz Lonegran in the Cowmobile, Somewhere, U.S.A.; Gene and Kathy Beaudry at Explorer Supply, South Burlington, Vermont; Terry Whitney in Westbrook, Maine; Susie Greer and Dusty the Dog at Elliott's Greenhouse, Stowe, Vermont; Jan and Blair Marvin in Johnson, Vermont; Henry Dunow, Tom Ettinger, and Roe Marra in New York; Phyllis Larkin, Cecilia Yung, and Connie Ftera at Macmillan; and Pam, Andrew, Sam, and the Guides at home. B.A.S.A.

Macmillan Publishing Company, 866 Third Avenue, New York, NY 10022. Collier Macmillan Canada, Inc. First Edition. Printed in the United States of America.

10 9 8 7 6 5 4 3 2 1

The text of this book is set in 13 point Criterion Light. The illustrations are black-and-white photographs reproduced in halftone.
The drawings on pages 22, 23, 30, 35, and 39, by Phil Benjamin and Lyn Severance, appear courtesy of Ben & Jerry's.
Jaspersohn, William. Ice cream / written and photographed by William Jaspersohn.—1st ed. p. cm.
Summary: Takes the reader on a tour of Ben and Jerry's ice cream plant to explain where ice cream comes from and how it is made.
ISBN 0-02-747821-1
1. Ice cream, ices, etc.—Juvenile literature. 2. Ice cream industry—Vermont—Juvenile literature. 3. Ben & Jerry's (Firm)—Juvenile literature.
[1. Ice cream, ices, etc. 2. Ben & Jerry's (Firm)] I. Title.   TX795.J37 1988   637′.4—dc 19   87-38331   CIP   AC

For Heinz Kluetmeier

Smooth and creamy, sweet and cold, ice cream is America's most popular dessert food. No country makes more ice cream than the United States, and no country eats more. Americans eat ice cream at an average rate of 15 quarts a year per person, and American factories produce ice cream at an annual rate of 923.6 million gallons. Over 10 per-cent of all the milk produced in the United States goes into making ice cream. It is a 3.9 billion-dollar-a-year business.

Americans love ice cream, but who makes it for them, and how? And how does it get from where it's made and into the hands of the people who eat it?

Some of the ice cream that Americans love to eat is made here, at the Ben & Jerry's ice cream plant in Waterbury, Vermont. The plant employs 150 people, who work five days a week making ice cream at a rate of 100,000 pints a day, 3.5 million gallons a year. The popularity of the product can be seen in the crowds that stream daily onto the grounds to buy their favorite flavors from the company's ice cream parlor, and to take the plant tour.

Much of the success of Ben & Jerry's as a company is due to the efforts of its founders, Ben Cohen and Jerry Greenfield. Ben and Jerry require that all the ingredients in their ice cream be fresh and of the highest quality, and that the chunks in their chunk-style ice creams be tasty, plentiful, and big. "We never use any artificial ingredients," says Jerry. "We could, but we wouldn't like the result." "What we're making," adds Ben, "is a super-premium ice cream. We want it to be the very best ice cream in the world."

3

To help ensure the high quality of their product, Ben & Jerry's buys its chief ingredients, milk and cream, from a nearby supplier, the St. Albans Cooperative Creamery. Dairy farmer George Pigeon, who lives in Georgia, Vermont, is a member of that cooperative, along with 474 other milk producers.

George milks his cows twice a day—at dawn, and twelve hours later. Every afternoon at 4:20 sharp, George, his son Morris, his grandson Chris, and the hired man Michael Gaudette drive George's 92 Holstein cows down from the pastures and into a low, wooden shed. From there, Michael and Morris let the cows into the milking parlor six at a time to be milked.

All the milking equipment works electronically, and the warm milk, fresh from the cows' udders, is automatically pumped into a stainless steel cooling tank in a room off the barn called the milk house.

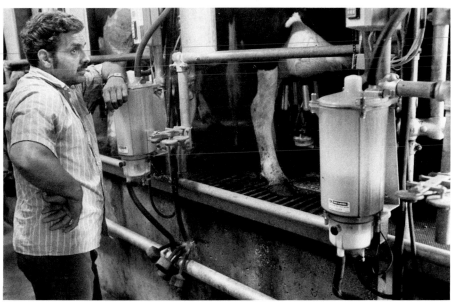

Three mornings a week, a tank truck arrives at the milk house to take the milk to the creamery. The driver, Tom Phillips, attaches a hose from the truck to the milk tank and then checks the measuring stick at the tank's top to see just how much milk there actually is. Today, there are 39.5 inches of milk in the tank, or over 900 gallons. Before starting the pump on the truck, Tom draws a small sample of milk into a glass vial for testing later at the creamery's laboratory.

Minutes later, after all the milk has been pumped from the tank, Tom hooks up the washing equipment, which automatically washes and rinses the tank for the next batch of milk from George Pigeon's cows that afternoon. By law, the creamery must refuse milk contaminated with disease-causing bacteria, so keeping the milking equipment clean is important.

At the St. Albans Cooperative Creamery, Tom gives the milk sample from the Pigeon farm to a lab technician, who checks it under a microscope for bacteria growth. Once the technician has okayed the milk, Tom can pump it into one of the creamery's six big storage silos.

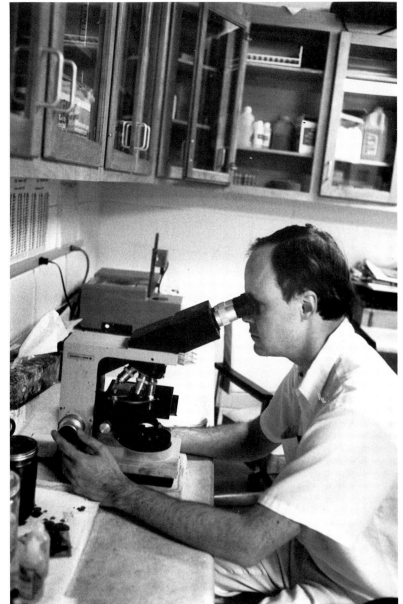

Within 24 hours the milk is piped into machines called centrifugal separators. The separators spin the raw product, causing part of it, called skimmed milk, to be thrown along the inside walls of the machine, and the other part, the cream, to rise up the machine's middle. The cream is then heated to kill bacteria that might have started growing in it, and the skimmed milk is moved into huge, six-story vacuum evaporators where it is steam-heated to remove some of its water. By the next day, two tank trucks, one holding 10,000 gallons of cream and the other an equal amount of skimmed, condensed milk, are on their way to Ben & Jerry's.

Meanwhile, another chief ingredient of Ben & Jerry's ice cream, cane sugar, is prepared for shipment at the Amstar refinery in Charlestown, Massachusetts. Sugar refining is an old business, dating back to the early 1700s. In the countries where it is grown, sugarcane, which is actually a species of grass, is cut into stalks and squeezed of its sweet, sugary juice. Boiling the juice causes its water to evaporate and the sugar in it to turn into small crystals.

Amstar receives this raw, crystallized sugar by ship from nations the world over: from the Dominican Republic, Mozambique, Madagascar, Mexico, Brazil, El Salvador, Fiji, Honduras—wherever sugarcane is grown. Amstar stores the raw sugar in a huge circular aluminum shed called the Dome.

Inside, the Dome is as big as a football field, and the sugar forms a mountain some 50 feet tall. Throughout the day and into the night, a big machine called a payloader moves the pale brown sugar onto conveyer belts that carry it into the refinery for processing.

11

After being washed of its protective molasses coating, which has kept the sugar from hardening into a single enormous lump, the sugar is dissolved in hot water, and the liquid, which is called sugar liquor, goes through a number of refining processes. It is clarified with phosphoric acid and lime, which helps start ridding it of impurities. It is filtered, first under pressure, in vats of filtering material called diatomaceous earth, then through towers filled with cattle bones that have been burned into charcoal and ground to the consistency of fine pebbles. Strange as these processes may seem, they all help to purify the sugar.

The light yellow sugar liquor is now sparkling clear and 99.9 percent pure. It is ready to be crystallized in vacuum vessels that heat the liquid, under vacuum, to 140 degrees Fahrenheit. Technicians watch the liquor closely, using special rods to draw small samples of it from the vessels. When the liquor is the consistency of thick slush, it is dropped into centrifuges one floor below. The inner wall of each centrifuge is lined with fine stainless steel mesh. The centrifuges spin the slush, and the syrupy part of it passes through the mesh, leaving the pure, crystallized sugar behind.

Later, this sugar is dried, melted in hot pure water, filtered yet again, and shipped in liquid form by truck to Ben & Jerry's.

When a tank truck full of sugar, cream, or condensed milk arrives at Ben & Jerry's, it is driven into a receiving bay, where a Ben & Jerry's worker pumps the ingredient out.

Cream and condensed milk are stored in tall refrigerated tanks in a chilly, narrow room called the tank room. Egg yolks, also essential for making high-quality ice cream, are kept in a freezer until needed. And ingredients that don't need refrigeration, such as sugar, which is pumped into its own tank, and cocoa, are stored in the company warehouse.

When the time comes to make a new batch of ice cream, a worker sets dials and pushes buttons on a big stainless steel switchboard. This causes precise amounts of sugar, cream, and condensed milk to flow into a shiny 1,000-gallon vat called a blend tank.

While the tank fills with these liquids, the worker lays out the necessary dry ingredients. These include cocoa, since this batch will be Chocolate ice cream, and a powder called stabilizer, which improves the ice cream's thickness and texture. Stabilizer is actually a mixture of two things: carrageenan, which comes from a seaweed called Irish moss, and guar gum, which comes from a plant grown in India.

While a blade in the blend tank stirs the soupy mix, the worker thickens it further with bucketfuls of egg yolks and bagfuls of cocoa. In all, he will pour into the tank some 40 gallons of egg yolks and 400 pounds of dried cocoa. All the ingredients combined will produce about 750 gallons of rich, chocolaty ice cream.

Once all the egg yolks, cocoa, sugar, cream, stabilizer, and condensed milk are thoroughly blended, the mix must be heated to rid it of any bacteria. Heating for this purpose is called pasteurization. The process is named after Louis Pasteur, the French doctor who invented it in 1864.

The pasteurizer looks a little like an old-fashioned steam radiator, and in a way that's how it works. Water-heated metal plates on one side of the pasteurizer quickly heat the ice cream mix to 183 degrees Fahrenheit and keep it at that temperature for 25 seconds, which kills any bacteria. After the mix has been further blended, water-cooled plates on the other side of the pasteurizer quickly chill it to 38 degrees Fahrenheit.

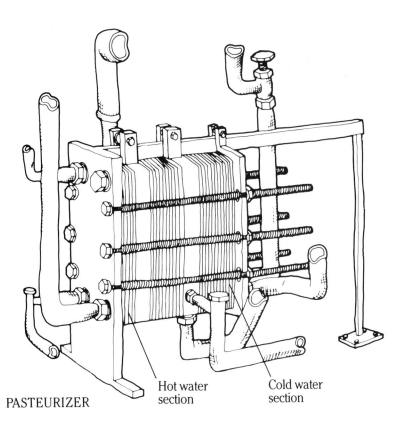

PASTEURIZER

Hot water section

Cold water section

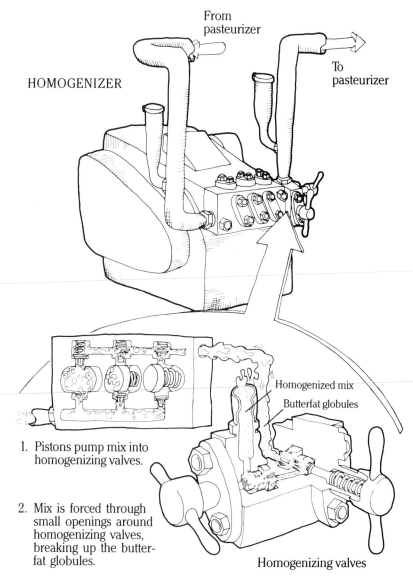

From pasteurizer

To pasteurizer

1. Pistons pump mix into homogenizing valves.

2. Mix is forced through small openings around homogenizing valves, breaking up the butterfat globules.

Homogenized mix

Butterfat globules

Homogenizing valves

The blending that occurs before the mix is chilled is called homogenization. The cream in the mix is filled with big globules of what ice cream makers and dairy people call butterfat. The homogenizer breaks up these fat globules by forcing the mix under high pressure through tiny valves. If the globules weren't broken up, they would float to the surface of the mix and ruin the finished ice cream. Homogenization, then, spreads the butterfat evenly through the mix, ensuring a smoother, better-tasting product.

19

Pasteurized and homogenized, the mix is now pumped into a storage tank where it ages at 38 degrees Fahrenheit for a minimum of four hours. Aging helps thicken the mix—the cream starts to harden and water swells the particles of stabilizer.

Four hours later, those mixes that require liquid flavorings are drawn into the flavor vat. There a worker adds precise amounts of such liquids as vanilla for Ben & Jerry's Vanilla ice cream and mint extract for their Mint with Oreo Cookies. You don't need much. Two gallons of vanilla, for example, are enough to flavor 300 gallons of mix.

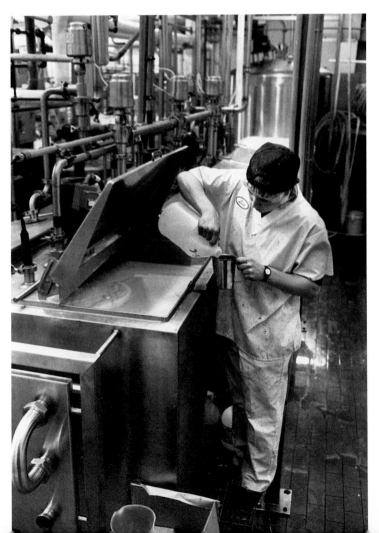

The mix is ready for perhaps its most important process: freezing. The ice cream freezer through which it now passes does two things at the same time: High-speed blades inside the freezer whip the mix, adding air to it; and chemical-filled metal coils around the whipping chamber freeze the water in the mix into tiny ice crystals. Both these steps are critical if the finished ice cream is to have the proper smoothness and texture.

In the company's quality control lab, trained technicians test the mix for butterfat content, freshness, and purity, checking to make sure that each mix is of the highest quality.

Here, too, new ice cream flavors are developed, tested, and sampled. The latest product on the market? Big, thick, chocolate-covered ice cream bars, which Ben and Jerry like to taste-test themselves.

Some mixes piped out of the freezer have dry ingredients, such as fruits and nuts, added to them. One of the most popular flavors is Heath Bar Crunch. The company buys the Heath Bar candy bars in boxes of 240 each. To prepare the bars for the ice cream, a worker lifts a boxful over his head and hurls it several times to the floor. This cracks the bars inside into bite-size bits and chunks.

When Ben and Jerry started their ice cream business, they broke the Heath Bars by dropping boxfuls of them off a stepladder. The hurling technique, they discovered, does the job faster and more easily.

Oreo cookies, for Mint with Oreo Cookies ice cream, come to the plant pre-broken.

All chunks, chips, cookies, nuts, and fruit for the ice cream are hand-scooped into a stainless steel hopper.

The hopper is attached to a machine called a fruit feeder, which blends the dry ingredients with the ice cream in controlled amounts. At 22 degrees Fahrenheit, the ice cream is soft enough to mix easily with the different kinds of chunks.

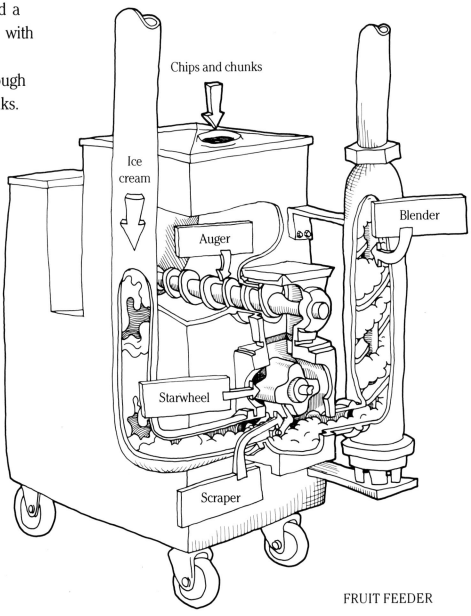

Chips and chunks

Ice cream

Auger

Blender

Starwheel

Scraper

FRUIT FEEDER

The ice cream is also soft enough to be packed in specially printed Ben & Jerry's pint-size containers. Pipes carry the finished ice cream from the freezer and the fruit feeder to workers who hand-pack it at a rate of about 40 pints a minute. Packing ice cream steadily over long periods can get boring, so packers work in short shifts.

Packers do other tasks as well, such as putting lids on the ice cream and fetching more pint containers from the warehouse.

At the same time, pipes also feed ice cream to the automatic filler, which can pack twice as fast as any worker. A dispenser drops pint cups into a metal ring, and a valve automatically fills each cup with ice cream as the cup is rotated underneath it.

Then a conveyer moves lids out of a bin, an arm automatically drops the lids in place on the filled cups, and another arm flips the lidded pint out of the ring. Another conveyer moves the pint on for further packaging.

Automation such as this means greater output. A single automatic filler can pack over 120,000 pints of ice cream in a single day.

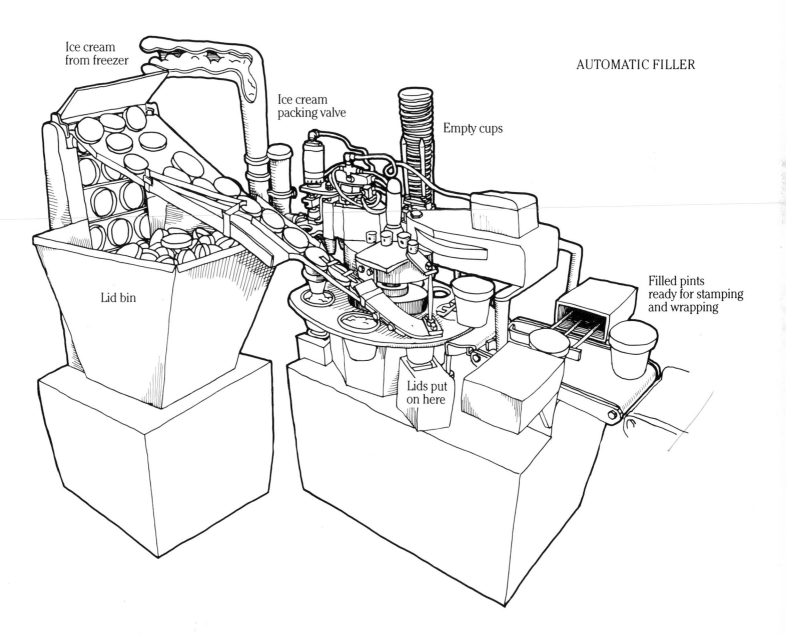

Ice cream
from freezer

Ice cream
packing valve

Empty cups

Lid bin

Filled pints
ready for stamping
and wrapping

Lids put
on here

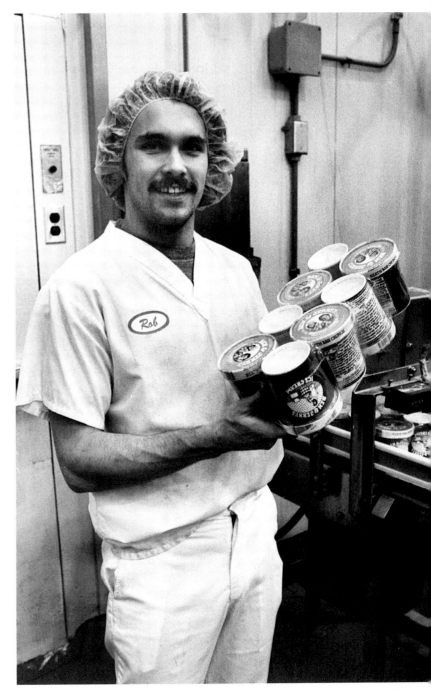

As the pints of fresh ice cream move along the conveyer, they pass over a printing machine that automatically prints two sets of numbers on each pint. One is the lot code, which is the number assigned to the particular batch. The other is the expiration date, or the last date that the ice cream should be sold. Properly frozen, Ben & Jerry's ice cream can be sold up until a year after it is made, so that is the date printed on the container.

After the pints are stamped, they are automatically wrapped in plastic in packs of eight for storage and shipping.

Sometimes, when the plant is particularly busy, Ben Cohen and Jerry Greenfield themselves help on the packing line. Today Jerry puts in some time on the line, hand-cleaning the pints before they are wrapped.

Two different flavors of ice cream have been made during this shift: Heath Bar Crunch and Chocolate. Throughout the packing procedure, the ice cream has been in a semisoft state at 22 degrees Fahrenheit. Now, however, it must be frozen hard so that it is fresh and tasty when it reaches consumers. How does Ben & Jerry's harden its ice cream?

An odd-looking freezing device is used. Twenty-five feet tall, it is called a spiral hardener. Packages of ice cream entering the bottom of the hardener on a conveyer are slowly drawn upward on a spiraling flexible belt. The air temperature inside the hardener room is minus 35 degrees Fahrenheit. With the windchill factor, thanks to the room's fans, the effective temperature is minus 60 degrees. Three hours after entering the hardener, the ice cream is brick hard and frozen solid.

SPIRAL HARDENER

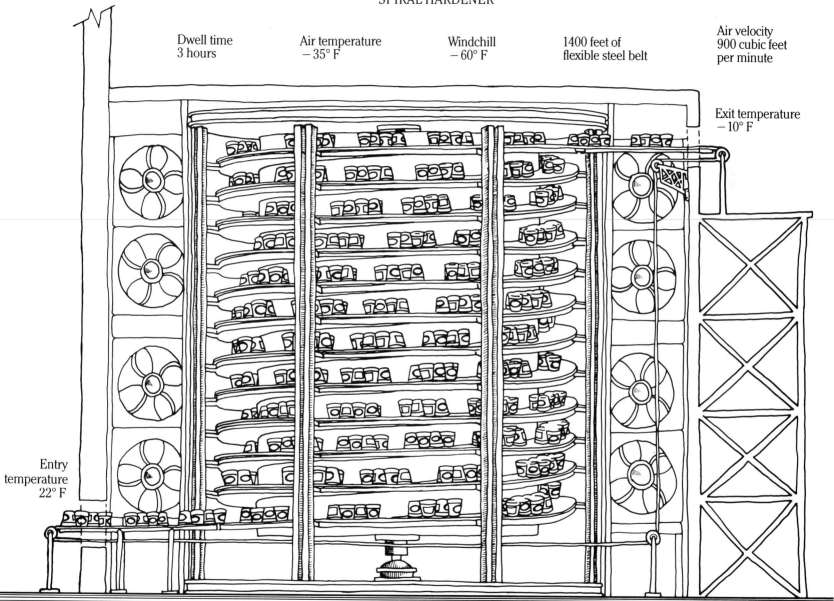

Dwell time
3 hours

Air temperature
− 35° F

Windchill
− 60° F

1400 feet of
flexible steel belt

Air velocity
900 cubic feet
per minute

Exit temperature
− 10° F

Entry
temperature
22° F

Now a conveyer moves the ice cream down from the top of the spiral hardener to a storage freezer. There a member of the Ben & Jerry's freezer crew stacks the ice cream on sturdy wooden pallets. Stacking in this fashion makes the ice cream easier to move by forklift.

The storage-freezer area, which can hold 1 million pints, is a slightly less chilly minus 10 degrees Fahrenheit. Company rules say that crewmen who work here must wear heavy hooded jumpsuits, warm boots, and mittens, and no one is allowed to remain in the area for more than an hour at a time.

Ice cream stays in the storage freezer no longer than ten days. In recent years, the demand for Ben & Jerry's ice cream has been so great that the company has had to work overtime to meet orders.

The man in charge of selling Ben & Jerry's ice cream to stores and supermarkets throughout the country is Rick Brown. He supervises a sales team that has found markets for the ice cream in 25 states nationwide. Stores in New York City alone buy 40,000 pints of Ben & Jerry's ice cream a day. Still, Rick will not be happy until the ice cream is selling in all 50 states.

To help spread the word about their product in new markets, Ben Cohen and Jerry Greenfield record radio commercials, make public appearances, give speeches, and pose for print advertisements. The company also sends a beautifully painted bus called a Cowmobile throughout the country to distribute free ice cream samples.

Such advertising and promotion efforts pay off. The more people know about Ben & Jerry's ice cream, the more they buy it. And the more they buy it, the bigger the company's profits are.

Twice a week, at seven o'clock in the morning, big refrigerator trucks roll up to the plant to pick up shipments of ice cream. Driver Terry Whitney waits as the temperature drops inside his truck's insulated trailer. When a gauge on its outside wall reads 0 degrees Fahrenheit, the trailer is cold enough to receive the ice cream.

Terry will drive the 5,000 pints of ice cream that he receives today to a main distributor in Conway, New Hampshire. In turn, the main distributor will ship the ice cream to secondary distributors, who will ship it to stores and supermarkets throughout the East. Distributors in other parts of the country follow the same procedure.

Ben & Jerry's has its own trucks and drivers for shipping ice cream to stores and restaurants in Vermont. The drivers work fast, wheeling the pints where they must go, but they always stack them carefully, in neat rows.

The last step in a process that started with raw ingredients happens now. People buy the ice cream, and the money they pay for it provides profits for the store, the distributors, and Ben & Jerry's. Profits are what keep companies alive, and a profitable company means jobs for many people.

Of course, nobody is supposed to think about these things when holding a fresh coneful of ice cream. Smooth and creamy, sweet and cold, ice cream isn't made to be thought about.

It's made to be eaten!